The Ascent

Drawing Closer to God

PETER GRANT

Illustrated by Emily Eggz

The Ascent

Onwards and Upwards Publishers
3 Radfords Turf,
Exeter,
EX5 7DX,
United Kingdom.
www.onwardsandupwards.org

Copyright © Peter Grant 2017

The right of Peter Grant to be identified as the author of this work has been asserted by the author in accordance with the Copyright, Designs and Patents Act 1988.

All rights reserved.

No part of this publication may be reproduced or transmitted in any form or by any means, electronic or mechanical, including photocopy, recording or any information storage and retrieval system, without permission in writing from the author or publisher.

This first edition published in the United Kingdom by Onwards and Upwards Publishers (2017).

ISBN: 978-1-911086-90-1
Typeface: Sabon LT
Illustrator: Emily Eggz / www.emilyeggz.com
Graphic design: LM Graphic Design

Printed in the United Kingdom.

Scriptures are taken from the Holy Bible, New International Version ®, NIV® Copyright © 1973, 1978, 1984, 2011 by Biblica, Inc.® Used by permission. All rights reserved worldwide.

About the Author

Peter is the Co-Director of Restored, an international Christian alliance dedicated to ending violence against women. Restored works with churches to prevent and respond to sexual and domestic abuse. Peter also leads Restored's "First Man Standing" campaign, which asks men to respect women and to challenge other men as to their attitudes and behaviour.

Peter was previously the International Director of Tearfund, with responsibility for its worldwide programmes. He has also been a Director for the UK Government's Department for International Development. His work and other travels have taken him to eighty countries around the world.

Peter is married to Stella. They met in Malawi, live in South London, where they are members of Streatham Baptist Church, and have two grown-up children. When their family was young, they lived for three years in Bangladesh, which remains close to their hearts. Peter is the author of *Poor No More* (Monarch, 2008), which outlines a Christian response to poverty.

Endorsements

This beautiful book is an easy read which draws you in and very soon you find yourself part of the story and being on the journey. The themes addressed are relevant and topical for each generation. The reflections and Bible verses given further cement our relationship with the story. This will make a great read for anyone who wants to spend time in communion with Christ. It will be great for new Christians and a real 'well' for those who have long been on the journey to drink from.

Rose Hudson-Wilkin
Priest in Charge of St Mary-at-Hill, London
Chaplain to the Speaker of the House of Commons and
Chaplain to the Queen

This is a powerful and intimate story of a journey. As I read it, I realised that, although it is Peter Grant's story, it is yours and mine as well. So many people are searching for a love that will not abandon them. *The Ascent* is a simple but profound guide to the love of God in Jesus and how we may grow as Christians.

Lord Carey
Former Archbishop of Canterbury

Any resource that helps me get closer to God gets my vote, so it's a thrill to recommend this book. It's inspirational yet practical too and does exactly what it says on the tin. Get two and give one to a mate.

Steve Legg
Editor, Sorted Magazine

This is a simple and delightful book where Peter's journey parallels our own and through it he invites us to walk with Jesus. It's a pleasure to read.

Rev'd Prebendary Mark Melluish
Senior Pastor, St Paul's Ealing & St Mellitus Hanwell
Assistant National Leader of New Wine

It is forty years since I committed my life to Jesus. As I read through *The Ascent*, familiar tears followed as the story echoed the longing to continue to walk closely with Jesus. The powerful simplicity of the Good News evokes a longing to draw ever closer. The amazing truth of acceptance, forgiveness, healing, restoration and calling are captured brilliantly in this story. No matter whether you have known Jesus for many years or are still to start the journey, I highly recommend you read *The Ascent* and work through the suggested applications, as in it you will find a refreshing joy. I look forward to meeting you on the slopes.

Sheryl Haw
International Director, Micah Global

The Ascent

Contents

Acknowledgements 8
Preface 9
PART ONE: THE STORY 11
1. The familiar voice 12
2. The hug 14
3. The changing room 16
4. The journey together 18
5. Stillness together 20
6. Eating and drinking together 22
7. The look 24
8. Worship 26
9. Commissioning and response 28
10. Sharing a vision 30
11. Union and communion 32
12. Together in battle 34
PART TWO: PUTTING IT INTO PRACTICE 37
1. A familiar voice 38
2. The hug 40
3. The changing room 42
4. The journey together 44
5. Stillness together 46
6. Eating and drinking together 48
7. The look 50
8. Worship 52
9. Commissioning and response 54
10. Sharing a vision 56
11. Union and communion 58
12. Together in battle 60
Author's Note 62

Acknowledgements

My thanks to my wife Stella for her love and encouragement and to all my friends who have commented on drafts.

A special thanks to the home group that I belong to at Streatham Baptist Church in London, ably led by Paul and Ros Tyas, who have helped me to know more about what it means to draw close to God.

Peter Grant

Preface

I had a great time at the "New Wine" Christian festival in the southwest of England during the summer of 2015. The highlight was a set of early morning Bible studies led by Charlie Cleverly about the Song of Songs. He has also published an excellent book on the subject, subtitled *Exploring the Divine Romance*[1]. The Song of Songs explores sexual passion and has been treated as an allegory of Christ's love for the church. But how does this apply to me in my relationship with Jesus? What does intimacy with God look like? And how can each of us draw closer to God in our daily lives?

My response to those questions is this fictional story. The book has twelve short chapters. Part 1 tells the story, with illustrations by Emily Eggz[2]. Part 2 includes a reflection on each chapter, a guide to help you apply it when you spend time with God and some Bible verses to meditate upon.

My aim is that, as you enter the story and imagine each scene for yourself, you will gain some insights to help you in your own personal devotional life. I have found that *The Ascent* has given me a structure for daily times with God and for longer periods with him. It has helped me to deepen my relationship with God. I pray that it will inspire you to draw closer to him and to know him better.

The words are mine and not those of Jesus. My aim is that they should reflect and be consistent with the Word of God in the Bible, and they should be judged on that basis.

I work with Restored[3], a Christian organisation committed to ending violence against women. It is in this context that my heart has been broken for what God sees when he looks down on the world. I am delighted that the royalties from this book will go towards the work of Restored.

---

[1] Charlie Cleverly, *The Song of Songs; Exploring the Divine Romance,* Hodder (2015)
[2] You can see more of Emily's illustrations at http://www.emilyeggz.com
[3] http://www.restoredrelationships.org

The Ascent

Part 1

The story

Who may ascend the mountain of the Lord?

Psalm 24:3

1

The familiar voice

I headed back the way I had come, looking for the sign. There it was.

The familiar voice

I had just parked my car when a message came through to say that the meeting had been cancelled. It was nine o'clock on a Monday morning, it was raining hard and I was a hundred and fifty miles from home. I turned the engine off and sat quietly, reflecting on my panic over the weekend to get my presentation sorted out, all for nothing.

The previous day some friends had prayed for me at church. They had a prophecy that Jesus wanted me "to join him up the mountain". It was a challenging image for me as a man whose work seemed to fill every corner of his life. Something stirred deep within me – a longing to be closer to God, to spend more time with him, to get back on track.

I decided to listen to his voice. I opened the bible that I kept in my car and started to read in Mark's Gospel where "Jesus took Peter, James and John with him and led them up a high mountain…"[4] Words and images rushed into my mind.

I heard Jesus saying, "Peter, I am the friend you hardly know. Come and spend time with me. Come up the mountain." My heart leapt as I recognised his voice, familiar from long ago.

"Where, Lord?" I asked. I remembered a sign just outside town pointing to a mountain lodge. I knew he would be there.

I turned the car round and headed back the way I had come, looking for the sign. There it was. I turned up the steep and narrow road, which gradually became more of a track as I approached the hills. The rain was easing off, but it was still a grey and misty day. I was not surprised that no one else was around as I parked my car and started the upward walk through the clouds. It was muddy and the climb was steep. I was in the wrong clothes.

---

[4] Mark 9:2

2

The hug

He threw his arms around me in a strong hug.

The hug

I could not see very far through the mist, but as I climbed, the light became brighter. Then suddenly the path emerged into brilliant sunshine. I blinked as I tried to take in the new world before me. Mountains rose into the distance, and all around white clouds moved slowly across a blue sky, revealing and then concealing other peaks and valleys.

I saw a figure running towards me. As he approached, I knew it was Jesus. He threw his arms around me in a strong hug. My clothes were wet and muddy. He didn't seem to care.

"Welcome. It's great to see you," he said. "I have waited a long time for this day." He didn't let go.

As the hug was held, I felt a deeper level of emotion. Slowly I put my arms around him and hugged him in return. We stayed that way for several minutes. Tears welled up, as I felt totally accepted and loved.

"My brother, my friend, I am so pleased that you are here," he said. "Let's journey up the mountain together."

There was nothing I wanted more.

The Ascent

3

The changing room

We jumped into the pool.

The changing room

A little way up the slope I saw a wooden building with a pool outside. Jesus held open the door. "You need to change those clothes," he said.

Inside was a gym and changing room. I took off my wet clothes and sat next to Jesus, on a bench, in my underwear. I felt vulnerable, conscious of my nakedness, unsure of what to do next.

"There are areas in your life we need to address," Jesus said, and I knew he was right.

Over the next half hour I poured out my sins and failures to him, sharing my doubts, confessing the many times I had let him down and the habits and addictive behaviours that so often controlled me. I acknowledged my neglect of prayer and relationships. I didn't want to hide anything. I knew I couldn't. "Is there anything else?" I asked, and he spoke of two deeper issues that needed to be dealt with.

At the end he looked me in the eye. "Your sins are forgiven;" he said, "now follow me and learn to live differently. I have some new clothes for you," he added, "but first let's take a swim."

We jumped into the pool. I felt clean and fully alive. I shouted out for joy and Jesus looked pleased.

"This is just the beginning," he laughed.

After a few minutes we got out and I put on the clothes he had laid out for me; simple and comfortable and with good shoes for walking. I wondered what lay ahead.

4

The journey together

We glimpsed the goats, deer and other animals that lived in the mountains.

"Where are we going?" I asked.

"Don't worry," said Jesus, "just follow me."

The next few hours were the most glorious of my life. Jesus and I climbed together and talked. I told him about my work, my worries, my hopes, dreams and disappointments. He encouraged me and explained the Bible to me, warming my heart with truth and insight. The pressure of work, so real just a few hours before, gradually lost its hold on me.

Sometimes the climb was tough. When I tripped and fell, he took my hand and helped me up. We scrambled up steep inclines and across narrow ridges, with steep drops on either side. In other places, the view opened out and we stopped to admire the beauty of creation together. From time to time we glimpsed the goats, deer and other animals that lived in the mountains. *You made all this,* I thought.

We sang, we laughed, we drank from a mountain stream. It was a holy pilgrimage. I expressed my thanks for all the good things in my life. I realised that Jesus was interested and involved in them all. I thought back on all the times I had faced tough situations on my own and so rarely spoken to him or brought him into my struggles. I knew I need never be alone again.

5

Stillness together

We stopped and sat in the apple tree's shade, side by side.

"Now we must find a place to rest and be still," Jesus said.

I felt strangely fearful. "I am not very good at being still," I confessed.

"I know," he said, and smiled.

Before us in the sunshine was a flat, grassy field with a stream running through it and, by the side of the stream, a huge apple tree. We stopped and sat in its shade, side by side. For ten minutes there was complete silence. At first I felt uncomfortable, but gradually my fear subsided.

Jesus leant across and breathed on me. "Receive my peace," he said.

I could feel a calm going deep into my spirit, sweeping away the anxiety. For the first time I could remember, I felt completely at rest.

"You have done most of the talking so far;" Jesus said, "I also want *you* to know *me* better." He spoke about what was on his heart; his sadness and joy; his hopes and concerns. He encouraged me to read and re-read the Bible, especially the Gospels, to know him better.

I felt my love for him deepen, as I understood more of his character and life. I grasped his hand and felt his firm grip. I dared to lean back on him, as John did at the Last Supper[5]. I could feel his heart beating.

"This is one of the most important things you will learn today," he said. "You must find times to be quiet with me each day, and you need to take a day of rest each week if you are going to sustain your journey. I want you to learn how to say no to some demands, so that you can create space for my priorities. All this takes practice, but I am always here to help you." He gave me the promise that he would order my time as I trusted him more. Then he breathed on me again. "Receive the Holy Spirit," he said. "He will teach you how to be still and to know me better."

---

[5] John 13:23-25

The Ascent

6

Eating and drinking together

Conversation flowed as we enjoyed the excellent food and wine.

We stood up and Jesus led me back to the path. Leaving the field behind us, we resumed our climb.

"It is time to think about the other people in your life," said Jesus. "Tell me about your family and friends."

I talked about all the people close to me and we prayed and gave thanks for each one. I thought about those who were far away from God and my eyes filled with tears. I looked across and saw that Jesus was weeping too.

Soon we saw the mountain lodge ahead of us. It turned out to be a huge banqueting hall. The meal was already underway with hundreds of men and women from many different nationalities sitting at the tables. The sight of the food made me realise how hungry I was.

"I want to introduce you to some of my other friends," said Jesus, leading me to a table with two spare seats. There were five other men around the table. I immediately recognised three of my closest friends, for whom we had just been praying. The other two I had never met.

They paused to welcome us warmly into their company. Jesus obviously knew each of them well. After brief greetings, he disappeared to re-emerge with plates piled high with food as he served us all our meals. Conversation soon turned to each man's story – honest, painful and full of challenge. I was struck by how Jesus was at the centre of each of their accounts. I felt excited to be with others who shared my faith in him. They asked me about my journey, which helped me to reflect on how God had been with me throughout my life, even when I wasn't aware of it.

Conversation flowed as we enjoyed the excellent meal. "None of you is on this journey alone," Jesus said. "You are my family and you need each other. I want you to be committed to each other; to love one another just as I love each of you."

We stopped to pray for each other and Jesus prayed for unity amongst us.

7

The look

It was a film of Jesus being crucified.

The look

As the meal finished, we shared bread and wine together. Jesus broke the bread and poured out the wine. The lights dimmed and I became aware that one of the walls of the hall was a giant screen. What was being projected captured the attention of everyone. It was a film of Jesus being crucified.

As I watched his suffering, my heart was broken by his love for the world. I looked across the table and noticed for the first time the nail scar on his wrist. I saw that he was looking deep into my eyes. It was a look that said, "This was not just for the world; this was for you. Amidst all these people, remember that I suffered and died for you." I returned his gaze.

I realised that I could know God, and not face the consequences of his judgement, only because Jesus had died for me. He had paid the penalty for my sins and I just needed to put my faith in him.

Of all the moments of the day, this was the most intimate. I bowed my head. "Thank you," I said quietly.

8

Worship

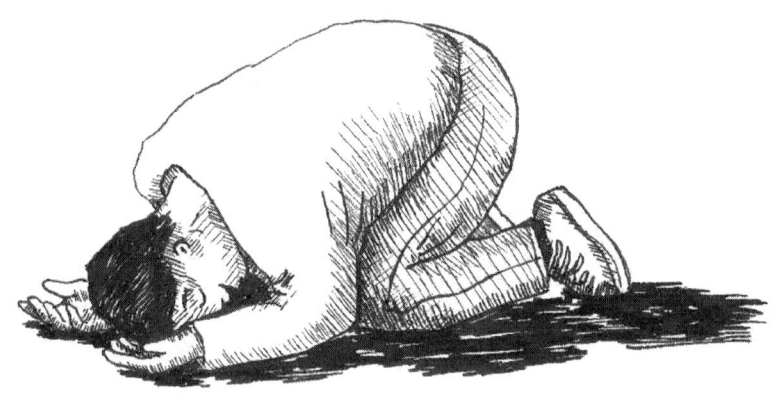

I fell face down on the floor in worship.

The movie continued through the sights and sounds of Jesus' burial on the Friday and into the quietness of Saturday at the tomb. The sense of expectation rose. Jesus had moved from our table to be at the front of the hall. Just before dawn broke on the Sunday, we watched on the film as Jesus rose from the dead with a great flash of light and the presence of angels. A mighty roar went up from the hall as everyone leapt to their feet to celebrate Jesus' resurrection and victory. We danced for joy together as music played and trumpets sounded.

"Follow me," Jesus called as huge doors opened behind him and we all poured out into a corridor leading to a higher and even greater chamber.

Out of this second room streamed the brightest light I had ever seen. My eyes adjusted slowly, but nothing prepared me to see God the Father on his throne, radiant in glory. As Jesus entered the room he also was transfigured. He went to sit at the right hand of the Father, his face shining as brightly as the sun, and the Holy Spirit filled the room with flames of fire.

I fell face down on the floor in worship. I could feel the cold of the stone floor against my forehead, and the blood coursing through my skull. I spoke out in every way I knew, my praise and my love to the Father and to Jesus. I shouted out loud and sang at the top of my voice.

I don't know how long I had been there, whether minutes or hours, when Jesus placed his hand on my shoulder and encouraged me to get up. I stood in awe and bliss.

The Ascent

9

Commissioning and response

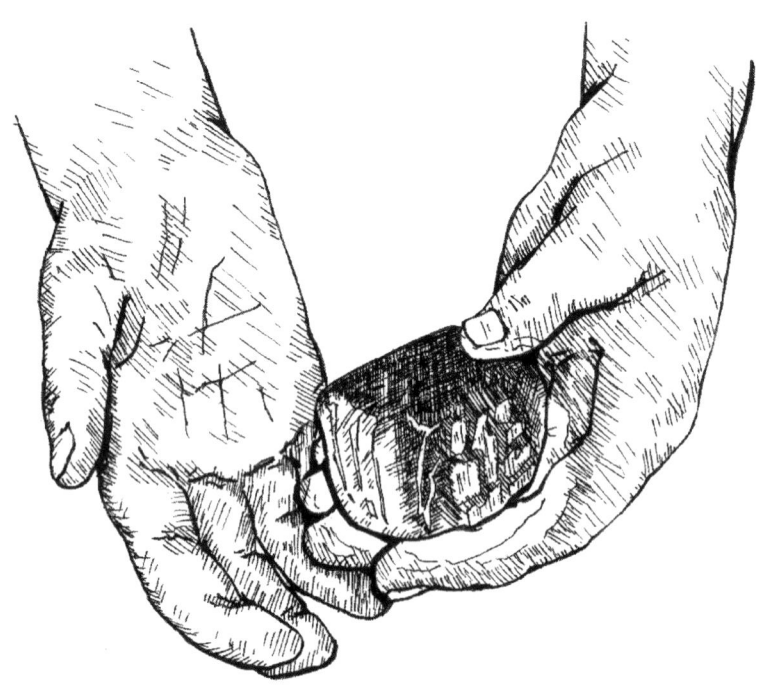

As the coal cooled down, he placed it in my hand.

There was silence in the room. Jesus spoke out in a loud voice and asked who would make a commitment to serve him wholeheartedly. I felt a touch of fear, but stepped forward along with many others.

Jesus took a hot coal from the fire and touched my forehead. "This coal represents God's purity which you must demonstrate in your life, and God's power to enable you to live for him." As the coal cooled down, he placed it in my hand. "Carry this as a reminder of your vow," he said.

Jesus beckoned me into a private room. I knelt in front of him and stretched out my arms. I opened my hands, the coal still held in my grip. "Lord, I give you my life. I surrender everything to you. What are you calling me to do?"

Jesus said, "I have significant plans for you. I have drawn you close to me so that you can show my love to others. You are not here just to know me, but to transform the world in my name. Be aware that this is going to be challenging. You must obey my commands. You will face opposition and persecution. You will need to give up much. Do you love me enough to pay this price?"

"I do," I said.

"Good," he replied, "I am pleased by your heart. This is not just a one-time commitment. You will need to renew it each day. Let's go and see what the Father and I have prepared for you to do."

The Ascent

10

Sharing a vision

Looking out, I could see the nations of the world below.

Jesus led me up a staircase and we stood before the Father in a round, unfurnished room. I realised that we were near the top of the mountain. After a while I became aware of the huge windows all around me. Looking out, I could see the nations of the world below. For the first time the Father spoke to me directly and asked me what was on my heart. We talked about my family and friends. I highlighted the issues and countries of the world that I cared about deeply and where I longed to see change. He told me of how he had placed these concerns in my heart and promised to make my vision and passion stronger. He spoke about my job and what he wanted to achieve through my everyday work.

He called me over to one of the windows. Wherever we looked, the cloud parted and we could see in detail what was happening on the earth below. We focused in on my road and neighbours and I sensed the Father's compassion for each person and his knowledge of the challenges faced by my community. As we zoomed in on other countries, we witnessed unspeakable poverty, persecution and suffering. I was given a small glimpse of what it is like for God to look down on the world he loves and to see each person's pain. I felt his anger against sin and injustice, but I also felt his joy and approval as we saw men and women, children and young people, loving and serving their communities courageously in his name.

"What is on *your* heart?" I dared to ask the Father. He spoke of his love for each person that he had made and his wish that none should perish. He explained his desire for justice and peace in the world and his purpose that all the nations should be blessed through Jesus. I felt my vision for serving God come alive and I was inspired to see the lives of brothers and sisters sacrificing so much to honour him.

"None of these acts goes unnoticed," Jesus said. He and I prayed and wept together for the people and situations that we had seen. He spoke to me of all that he had prepared for me to do for him. "You will speak of me and show my love to many people," he said.

I felt daunted but excited.

The Ascent

11

Union and communion

I was amazed to see a room marked with my name.

"Come with me into one final room," said Jesus, "and spend some time with us. This is the pinnacle of your Ascent."

I followed Jesus up a short staircase and into the presence of all three members of the Trinity – the Father, Jesus and the Holy Spirit, who hovered over both as a dove. I stood alone with the Triune God, the fulfilment of all my hopes and longing. I watched in awe and reverence as the Trinity related to each other in love and mutual honour. It was beyond understanding.

I felt that over the past few hours I had come to know something of Jesus as my brother, my friend and my Lord. I could imagine him walking alongside me throughout my life's journey. But how was I to relate to the Father and to the Holy Spirit?

Jesus knew my thoughts. "The Father loves you and knows everything about you, including all your sadness and grief, down to the smallest detail," he said. "Speak to him as your dear and loving father. Call him Dad if you feel comfortable to do so, and don't hesitate to bring him all your problems and needs."

"And how should I relate to the Holy Spirit?" I asked.

"He is living within you to help build your character to be more like me," Jesus said. "He will remind you of my words and give you power to be effective. He will fill you with the compassion and courage you will need each day. He is always ready to be your guide and helper, especially as you read the Bible. You can call on him whenever you need direction or strength."

I looked up and was amazed to see a room marked with my name. "Is this for me?" I asked.

"Not yet," Jesus replied, "but one day it will be your home forever."

I realised that my yearning for relationship with God would one day be completely fulfilled. I longed to stay and enjoy more of this union and communion with the Trinity. I could hardly bear to leave, but I knew I must.

12

Together in battle

Jesus showed me photos of perhaps twenty other men and women.

"It is time to return," Jesus said. "You are going back to a battle where the fighting will be fierce. You know me now, but you will know me in an even deeper way as we stand shoulder to shoulder against the enemy. You will face battles to overcome sin in your life; to endure persecution and suffering; to maintain unity within the church; and to share my good news through words and acts of love." He prayed for me again – for compassion and courage, for purity and power, and for the Holy Spirit to fill me. "Pray this prayer and commit your life afresh to me each day," he said.

Jesus led me out of the room and down a corridor. "Hold firm to the promises that I have given to you in the Bible. Learn them and rely on them. Always remember that you are part of my team and not alone," he said, smiling. I looked up and saw the other five men from the table now joining me for the return journey. Jesus showed me photos of perhaps twenty other men and women. Some were already familiar to me, others not. "They will all become true friends," he promised.

We walked out of the building together as a group and down the path.

"Can I come back here again?" I asked.

"Not until you die or I return," Jesus replied, "but you can recreate this journey as often as you want in your mind, and I will be there with you."

As we approached the cloud level, he hugged me once again and slipped a piece of paper into my pocket alongside my piece of coal.

I reached the car park and waved goodbye to my friends, promising to meet again soon.

I returned home and some said my face was glowing. My phone had a huge number of unanswered messages, people wondering where I had been. There were several mini-crises that needed to be addressed.

I opened the paper. It read, "I love you. I am with you. I will never leave you nor forsake you."

I wept with joy.

The Ascent

Part 2

Putting it into practice

*Reflections, applications
and verses from the Bible*

1

A familiar voice

It is always good to answer the phone and hear the voice of someone you love. Over time we learn to recognise a voice from even the shortest snatches of speech. But instant recognition is not without its risks. When I started going out with my wife, Stella, she shared a flat with her sister, who had a very similar voice. When I called on the house phone that they shared, I had to be careful to check I had the right sister before I opened my heart to her!

When God introduces himself to someone in the Bible, or speaks to them for the first time, he often displays his knowledge of their character and origins. He also frequently reveals something about himself – his name or his vision for a specific task. See, for example, the calls of Abraham, Moses, Gideon, Isaiah, Jeremiah, Nathaniel and Paul[6].

God loves to communicate with us and he wants us to seek after him. The rush of life often leaves little space for God. We are so easily distracted. In the midst of life's other voices, the voice of God can be quiet, but it is distinctive. Jesus promises we will recognise it. He calls us to come away and spend time with him. Are we listening?

APPLICATION

If you are going to make the Ascent, you must listen to God, give time to him and learn how to recognise his voice. You need to bring a hunger and thirst for him, or at least the desire to be hungry and thirsty. He will do the rest. Start by reading the Bible, which helps you to know

---

[6] Bible references for God's call: Abraham (Genesis 12), Moses (Exodus 3), Gideon (Judges 6), Isaiah (Isaiah 6), Jeremiah (Jeremiah 1), Nathaniel (John 1:47-51) and Paul (Acts 9).

God better and to understand his thoughts. The Holy Spirit will help you to discern and hear his voice as you read.

Ask people to pray for you and, if they have the gift, to prophesy over you. Try studying those passages in the Bible when God calls people and speaks to them one-to-one. What do you learn about him and his intimate knowledge of each individual? Make time to go away and be alone with God.

Why not pause right now and listen? What is God saying? Can you recognise his voice? It requires a decision to respond. Be assured that God wants to pursue a relationship with you and that he will be there to meet you. He may have been waiting a long time for this day. Listen for his voice and start to make the Ascent towards knowing him better. Get rid of distractions. Open your bible and ask God to speak.

SOME BIBLE VERSES TO MEDITATE ON

I lift my eyes to the mountains – where does my help come from? My help comes from the Lord, the maker of heaven and earth.

Psalm 121:1-2

Come, let us go up to the mountain of the Lord, to the house of the God of Jacob.

Micah 4:2

The Lord said to Moses "Come up to me on the mountain..."

Exodus 24:12

The friend who attends the bridegroom waits and listens for him, and is full of joy when he hears the bridegroom's voice.

John 3:29

His sheep follow him because they know his voice.

John 10:4

2

The hug

The Ascent begins with a hug, which is an expression of God's love and acceptance before we have said or done anything. Jesus loves us as we are and not on the basis of our performance. We will need to deal with our failures and requests at some stage, but each time we meet Jesus we can first of all experience the warmth of his embrace. He loves us. Just like the father in the parable of the Prodigal Son[7], Jesus runs to meet us and to hug us. He is not concerned about his dignity.

The length of a hug matters. A brief hug is an expression of greeting and affection. As it is held, it allows for a much deeper range of emotions. The father of the Prodigal Son invested years of emotion in that hug. God feels the same way towards each of us.

APPLICATION

The Bible encourages you to seek after God in the knowledge that he is also seeking after you. Can you imagine Jesus running towards you to hug you? Can you see the expression of love and acceptance in his eyes?

What do you do first when you enter God's presence? Is it to confess your sins, to ask for something or to praise him? I suggest that, first of all, you imagine Jesus giving you a hug. This is regardless of whether you deserve it or not. God's love is not dependent on how we feel about ourselves. Why not also try imagining this each day when you wake up?

The length of the hug and its intensity will depend on your situation and level of need. Maybe you need a long hug from Jesus right now. Realise afresh that God loves you. He always has. He always will. So don't be in a rush.

---

[7] Luke 15:11-32

SOME BIBLE VERSES TO MEDITATE ON

Look! Here he comes, leaping across the mountains, bounding over the hills.

Song of Songs 2:8

While he was still a long way off, his father saw him and was filled with compassion for him; he ran to his son, threw his arms around him and kissed him.

Luke 15:20

Therefore, there is now no condemnation for those who are in Christ Jesus ... If God is for us, who can be against us?

Romans 8:1,31

How great is the love the Father has lavished on us that we should be called children of God! And that is what we are!

1 John 3:1

For I am convinced that neither death nor life, neither angels nor demons, neither the present nor the future, nor any powers, neither height nor depth, nor anything else in all creation, will be able to separate us from the love of God that is in Christ Jesus our Lord.

Romans 8:38-39

3

The changing room

There is something about stripping off and sitting together in a changing room that allows for intimacy of conversation. Our local gym has a men's sauna where I love to sit during cold winter evenings with a group of men who gather just before closing time. Most conversations revolve around sport, but just occasionally we touch on deeper things and the sauna becomes a sacred space.

Nakedness speaks of vulnerability. God sees us as we really are and it is a huge relief to be honest and fully confess our sins to him. That is why I find the changing room such a good picture of confession, especially when linked to changing our clothes and diving into a pool or shower that speaks of cleansing and release.

APPLICATION

As you set out on the Ascent, get rid of all the sin that hinders you and drags you down. Imagine sitting with Jesus in a changing room. You may well feel vulnerable and ashamed, but how much better to be open with the one who can forgive and cleanse you, than to run and hide without any hope of change. Speak out all your sins to Jesus; he knows them anyway. Allow Jesus to search your heart and point out any other issues you need to address. Don't try to avoid responsibility, but rather ask for forgiveness and for your sin to be dealt with.

As you confess your sins, turn away from them and accept his forgiveness deep in your heart. This is why he came to Earth – so that you could be completely free from sin and without guilt. His cross makes forgiveness and cleansing available to us at any time and in full measure. Live in that truth and reality. Celebrate it. Shout it out. Thank Jesus, as you shower or swim, for his forgiveness, cleansing and new life. Put on your new clean clothes. You are ready to climb higher.

SOME BIBLE VERSES TO MEDITATE ON

Who may ascend the mountain of the Lord? Who may stand in his holy place? The one who has clean hands and a pure heart.

Psalm 24:3-4

If you, O Lord, kept a record of sins, O Lord who could stand? But with you there is forgiveness; therefore you are feared.

Psalm 130:3-4

If we confess our sins, he is faithful and just and will forgive us our sins and purify us from all unrighteousness.

1 John 1:9

You have taken off your old self with its practices and have put on the new self, which is being renewed in knowledge in the image of its Creator.

Colossians 3:9-10

Let us throw off everything that hinders and the sin that so easily entangles, and let us run with perseverance the race marked out for us.

Hebrews 12:1

4

The journey together

Friendships are forged by shared experiences. I have friends whom I have got to know much more deeply when on international trips together. Jesus is the best of all friends. I can tell him everything as he and I share the journey of life together each day.

The image of a walk with Jesus is a powerful one, especially when it involves times of danger, challenges to overcome and beauty to share. A challenging climb in beautiful mountain scenery following the Creator of the universe is a picture of how we can journey with Jesus every day of our lives. The recollection that he stands by our side is an encouragement in hard times, a shared joy in good times and a very practical deterrent to sin.

Previous generations have encouraged us to "practise the presence of God". This means being aware of him throughout the day and involving him in all we do. I love the idea of my life being an adventure with Jesus. Sharing my experiences of daily life whether profound or mundane. Seeking his help when times are tough. Finding out that in him I have a friend who is indeed closer than a brother.

APPLICATION

Jesus invites you to follow him and to trust him that he knows the way. Bring him consciously to mind as you go about your daily life. Invite him to share a beautiful view, to wrestle with a problem you face or to share the depths of illness and bereavement. Parents never tire of hearing the stories that their children tell them about the smallest details of their daily life. In times of prayer, tell Jesus about everything that is happening to you and how you feel about it. He really is interested in the mundane as well as the dramatic. Each morning you can commit your day to God by imagining Jesus in each of the situations you will enter, and review the previous day with him by reflecting on how he was with you in all you went through.

Be conscious of Jesus walking alongside you in the different challenges of danger and temptation. Share with him your joys and celebrations. Give thanks for all the good things that he has given to you. The antidote to jealousy and discontent is an appreciation of the wonderful privileges that we have in being alive and the gifts that God showers on us every day. Give space in each of your times of prayer for giving thanks and listing the good things that you appreciate in your life.

SOME BIBLE VERSES TO MEDITATE ON

"I am with you," declares the Lord.

Haggai 1:13

There is a friend who sticks closer than a brother.

Proverbs 18:24

Were not our hearts burning within us while he talked with us on the road and opened the Scriptures to us?

Luke 24:32

Cast all your anxiety on him because he cares for you.

1 Peter 5:7

Give thanks in all circumstances, for this is God's will for you in Christ Jesus.

1 Thessalonians 5:18

5

Stillness together

This was always going to be the hardest, but perhaps most precious, part of the Ascent for me. When I arrive home, and no one is there, my first instinct is always to turn on the radio or TV, to fill the space with news or sport and to eat and drink. I am slowly learning that my greatest need is not to fill my silence with noise, or to get to the bottom of my to-do list, but to be still and at peace with Jesus.

Why do I find stillness so hard? Partly it is because of the distractions around me which are so numerous and insistent. Stillness requires commitment and perseverance and is an area where the saints of ages past, who practised the disciplines of silence and meditation, have much to teach us.

It is in the quietness that we can switch our attention from ourselves to Jesus. It is here that we remember that intimacy is as much about us getting to know Jesus as it is about us pouring out our issues and needs to him. Sometimes it is good to spend time in prayer with Jesus, meditating on his words, with no agenda but just a desire to be with him and to hear what he is saying to us.

APPLICATION

Stillness and peace in the presence of God are precious. God invites you to spend time quietly with him. What are the barriers that prevent you from doing so?

God knows you. How well do you know him? Spending time meditating on God's word is vital if you want to know him in a more intimate way. Can you take ten minutes each day to be silent, to read a few verses from one of the Gospels and to listen to God's voice? Or set aside a specific time each week to be silent with him? Pray the prayer of Samuel: "Speak, Lord, for your servant is listening."[8]

Pray to be filled with Jesus' peace and the Holy Spirit each day. Ask God to order your time. Are there things you should be saying no to, so that you can focus on his priorities? Are you taking a day off each week as a time in which you can stop work and concentrate on him?

SOME BIBLE VERSES TO MEDITATE ON

Come to me, all you who are weary and burdened, and I will give you rest.

Matthew 11:28

Come with me by yourselves to a quiet place and get some rest.

Mark 6:31

Peace I leave with you; my peace I give you.

John 14:27

Be still and know that I am God.

Psalm 46:10

He makes me lie down in green pastures, he leads me beside quiet waters, he restores my soul.

Psalm 23:2-3

---

[8] 1 Samuel 3:9-10

6

Eating and drinking together

We are not meant to live life or serve God on our own. The Bible talks about the church as a body, with many different and mutually dependent parts. I am very conscious of my own strengths and weaknesses, but often find it hard to reach out to others for help and partnership. Relationships of trust and co-operation are vital if we are to be effective in living for God.

I am privileged to have a loving family and supportive friends. Over the past few years I have consciously invested in trying to spend more time with a number of my close male friends. God challenges me to pray for my friends and family as one of the key ways I can affect the world.

Eating is enjoyable, but eating together is hugely more so. I never liked staying in hotels on business trips when I had to eat alone. Jesus puts us in teams, and eating and drinking together is a great way to build our team, to plan, reflect and celebrate. Jesus often describes the Kingdom of God as a great feast characterised by joy and celebration. It is possible both to have fun and to make a big impact; in fact, the two often go together.

APPLICATION

Are you trying to do too much on your own? I encourage you to invest significant time in your family and in a small number of close friendships that will provide real support, challenge and accountability. What do you need to stop doing in order to prioritise your relationships?

This part of the Ascent provides an opportunity for you to pray for your family, your friends and your teams. Bring to mind those who are close to you. Pray and give thanks for each of them. Imagine Jesus in the midst of all your relationships. Thank God for the men and women who inspire you, whom God has placed alongside you on your journey.

Many friendships are built around shared interests or a common passion and can form the nucleus of teams that accomplish great things for God. Give thanks for the teams that you are part of and reflect on new areas where God may be calling you to work with others.

Do you look out for opportunities to share meals with friends? Why not invite lonely people to join you? Jesus loves parties. Imagine him serving at your table or washing your feet. How can you serve others and show humility in a similarly radical way? Generous hospitality, especially to people who are different from you, is a great adventure, full of unexpected joy and fulfilment.

SOME BIBLE VERSES TO MEDITATE ON

If anyone hears my voice and opens the door, I will come in and eat with him and he with me.

Revelation 3:20

Now that I, your Lord and teacher, have washed your feet, you also should wash one another's feet.

John 13:14

Love one another. As I have loved you, so you must love one another.

John 13:34

Keep on loving each other as brothers. Do not forget to entertain strangers.

Hebrews 13:1-2

When you give a banquet, invite the poor, the crippled, the lame, the blind and you will be blessed.

Luke 14:13-14

7

The look

A look can say so much. A look from my wife across a crowded room speaks of knowledge and intimacy in a public place. Looks can express powerful emotions. I try to imagine how Jesus looked at Peter after he had denied him three times[9]. To look someone in the eyes is to be unashamed of being in relationship with them. Jesus looks at each of us with love.

This is the most intimate part of our relationship with Christ. Taking bread and wine reminds us that he died on the cross for each of us. It is only because he has paid the penalty for my sins that I can know God and approach him with confidence. I can only imagine what it will be like in heaven when I see him face to face and he looks into my eyes.

APPLICATION

We can focus on Jesus' death in many ways, including through communion, through the image of the sacrificial lamb or through the word pictures painted in the New Testament. Some find an image of Jesus on the cross to be helpful in focussing on what he has done for us. Others do not. The fact that Jesus has kept his wounds in his resurrected body, and that he established the bread and the wine as a specific memorial of his death, point to the importance of us reflecting upon his death for us on the cross. This is the centre of our faith.

What ways do you find it easiest to reflect on Jesus' death on the cross for you? Spend some time meditating and thanking him for his love for you as shown on the cross. Imagine Jesus looking at you now and you at him. Hold the gaze. How do you feel? Thank him for his

---

[9] Luke 22:61

love and sacrifice for you. What does it mean to you that one day you will see him face to face?

SOME BIBLE VERSES TO MEDITATE ON

My heart says of you "Seek his face!" Your face, Lord, I will seek.

Psalm 27:8

You have stolen my heart with one glance of your eyes.

Song of Songs 4:9

Christ died for sins once for all, the righteous for the unrighteous, to bring you to God.

1 Peter 3:18

God shows his own love for us in this: While we were still sinners, Christ died for us.

Romans 5:8

Now we see but a poor reflection as in a mirror; then we shall see face to face. Now I know in part; then I shall know fully, even as I am fully known.

1 Corinthians 13:12

8

Worship

Every Sunday is a celebration of Jesus' resurrection and an occasion for praise. Sometimes, especially in a small church, our praise can feel muted, but we are all part of the huge worldwide church praising God. One of the privileges of going to a big Christian conference is being able to worship in a large crowd with other voices and instruments as an anticipation of heaven.

God is worthy of our praise. He is glorious and on his throne. Three of the disciples saw Jesus transfigured in his glory and now, following his death and resurrection, he is at the right hand of the Father in heaven. It is right for us to bow down before him. Bowing speaks of respect and honour – the deeper the bow, the greater the submission. Many important people on earth become accustomed to having people bow to them, but worshipping God is altogether different. It is the only appropriate response to who God is and who we are.

Worship is intimacy. Worship leaders are often those from whom we can learn most about intimacy with God. I don't find that worship comes naturally to me and I seldom think about my posture in worship. But there is something very visceral about kneeling down and putting my forehead on the floor. The blood rushes to my head. I feel the pressure of the ground. I am vulnerable and exposed and unable to see around me. The physical act creates the occasion for me to speak out my love and praise to God.

APPLICATION

This chapter encourages you both to worship God in a crowd and on your own. Seek out places where you can shout out, dance and sing your praise in the company of others. And when you are on your own in worship there are no constraints. No one is watching. You can do whatever you want. In your time with God, read some of the descriptions of God's glory and his throne and worship him.[10] Meditate on the occasions in the Bible where we see Jesus glorified – in the transfiguration[11] and in heaven, in the Book of Revelation[12]. Reflect on what it means that your friend and brother, Jesus, is also the glorious Lord of the universe.

Think of Jesus taking his three closest friends with him up the mountain so that they could see his transfigured glory. Imagine you were with them. Bow down with your face to the floor and worship him. Speak out your praise in an audible voice; shout if you feel comfortable to do so. Express your love to him. Practise now for what awaits you in heaven.

SOME BIBLE VERSES TO MEDITATE ON

Great is the Lord and most worthy of praise in the city of our God, his holy mountain.

Psalm 48:1

Jesus took Peter, James and John with him and led them up a high mountain, where they were all alone. There he was transfigured before them.

Mark 9:2

Thomas said to him, "My Lord and my God!"

John 20:28

When they saw him, they worshipped him, though some doubted.

Matthew 28:17

His face was like the sun, shining in all its brilliance. When I saw him, I fell at his feet as though dead. Then he placed his right hand on me and said, "Do not be afraid."

Revelation 1:16-17

---

[10] For example, Ezekiel 1:4-28 and Revelation 4:2-11
[11] Mark 9:2-8
[12] Revelation 1:12-18

9

Commissioning and response

People are looking for something to live for and something worth dying for. Although we often choose comfort and ease, deep within we are longing for a challenge, for the knowledge that we have not wasted our lives on things that don't matter. Jesus offers us this opportunity. He never waters down the sacrifices or the risks. Rather, he lets the desire grow in our hearts so that we are eager and willing to follow, whatever the cost.

The coal is a symbol of God's initiative both to commission us and to equip us with purity and power for the task. Our response is to offer our whole lives, counting the cost and holding nothing back. This commitment is just a beginning. I am learning that persistence and faithfulness are two of the most important characteristics of an effective follower of Jesus. I have promised my all to Jesus in the past, but he also calls me daily to renew my commitment to him.

APPLICATION

Following Jesus wholeheartedly is a decision of the heart. Jesus calls you to live an extraordinary life for him, and to lay down all that you have and are in his service, including your money, your time and your longing for recognition.

Are you willing to answer his call and totally submit to Jesus? Have you counted the cost?

The commission is always his initiative. He calls you personally and you need to respond in that private place with him alone. Ask for his touch of fire to equip you with purity and power in your life. Why not find a piece of coal to remind you of your calling?

God always has new possibilities for your life. Each day needs to be a fresh submission to God. Will you follow him again today, perhaps despite all that you have been through? Will you accept his discipline and re-engage with the battle against sin in your life and the challenges of the world? Will you share his good news with others, serving the poor and speaking out for those who have no voice? It is at the deepest level of commitment that we find the deepest level of intimacy.

SOME BIBLE VERSES TO MEDITATE ON

> *Then I heard the voice of the Lord saying, "Whom shall I send? And who will go for us?" And I said, "Here am I. Send me!"*
>
> Isaiah 6:8
>
> *I chose you and appointed you so that you might go and bear fruit – fruit that will last.*
>
> John 15:16
>
> *I urge you … to offer your bodies as living sacrifices, holy and pleasing to God.*
>
> Romans 12:1
>
> *Any of you who does not give up everything he has cannot be my disciple.*
>
> Luke 14:33
>
> *Whatever was to my profit, I now consider loss for the sake of Christ.*
>
> Philippians 3:7

10

Sharing a vision

God gives us the privilege of sharing his vision for the world and drawing us in to its fulfilment. Our life's calling will always reflect something that is important to him. God cares about our families, our neighbours and our friends. He is able to take our everyday work and weave it into his plan.

It is hard to imagine how God feels when he looks down on the world. My work towards ending violence against women has challenged me to reflect on the epidemic of domestic and sexual abuse, forced marriage and other violence that affects one in three women around the world. What does God's love mean for a woman suffering domestic abuse in rural Bangladesh or a woman raped in the Democratic Republic of Congo? God sees and weeps and he will hold those who perpetrate violence to account.

And yet there is also hope. God sees the stories of faith and heroism that never reach the newspapers. He is full of pride and joy when his children serve others in his name. He records every act of love and generosity and they will not be forgotten. He is at work through us to change the world he loves. He calls on us to pray to him and with him for the situations and people on our heart.

APPLICATION

What are you passionate about? What's your life's calling under God? Will you "let your heart be broken by things that break the heart of God"[13]? Talk to him about the people and issues that you care about and let him fan into flame those desires, ideas and plans. Dare to ask him to share his heart with you and catch you up in his purposes. Invite him into your work situation and allow him to transform your

---

[13] Bob Pierce, Founder of World Vision

Sharing a vision

perspective. What does he want to do in partnership with you over the next five years? Pray and plan. Get excited.

This is also the opportunity on the Ascent to pray for the needs of the world. Pray for your family, neighbours and friends to come to know Jesus. Pray for God's purposes of justice and peace to be brought about in the world. Pray for those countries and situations where poverty, persecution and suffering are at their worst. Pray for things to change and expect God to answer.

The Ascent can never just be about our love for God and his love for us. It must flow out to the world. You can bring God pleasure by being part of his response to the needs that you encounter. He has prepared good works in advance for you to undertake. He wants you to pray and bring in as much of his kingdom on earth as you can. Make sure you don't miss out on sharing his vision for you and for the world.

SOME BIBLE VERSES TO MEDITATE ON

For God so loved the world that he gave his one and only Son, that whoever believes in him shall not perish but have eternal life.

John 3:16

We are God's workmanship, created in Christ Jesus to do good works, which God prepared in advance for us to do.

Ephesians 2:10

The Lord loves righteousness and justice.

Psalm 33:5

He is patient with you, not wanting anyone to perish, but everyone to come to repentance.

2 Peter 3:9

Pray continually.

1 Thessalonians 5:17

11

Union and communion

We think too little of heaven.

This chapter goes way beyond my experience, but is based on God's certain promise of all that lies ahead for each of us who trust in him. It speaks of the personal place that God has reserved for me in heaven. It affirms the reality that, with God, the best is always yet to come.

As a child, growing up before the information revolution, the idea that God could know everything about everyone seemed unimaginable. Now even man-made computers know an extraordinary level of detail about the lives of hundreds of millions of people. God knows the number of hairs on our heads and cares passionately about every aspect of our lives. He knows about my joys and successes; my suffering and sadness; my pain and bereavements. I can relate to him on that basis as my loving heavenly Father, my Dad.

Relating to the Holy Spirit feels more difficult. We are encouraged to be filled with the Holy Spirit and to keep in step with him. He lives within us to help us be transformed into the likeness of Jesus and to bear spiritual fruit. He equips us with his gifts, strength and courage. He is also alongside us and I can relate to images of the Holy Spirit as my guide and helper. When I switch on my phone, my "intelligent personal assistant" asks me if I need any help. The Holy Spirit is infinitely more present, more knowledgeable and more powerful than my phone.

Application

This chapter speaks of a longing for eternity that God plants in your heart. Pray that you will hunger more and more to live in the presence of God; Father, Son and Holy Spirit. The New Testament writers had an eager expectation of Christ's return and being with him forever. This is closer now than when they first wrote.

How do you relate to each member of the Trinity? Imagine your life's journey with Jesus walking alongside you, the Father as your heavenly Dad to whom you can bring all your needs, joys and sorrows and the Holy Spirit both within you and at your side to be your guide and helper. Consciously bring your needs to the Father each day. Remember the presence of Jesus in your life, especially when you face temptation or experience joys or hardships. And why not be prompted to recall that the Holy Spirit is with you every time you pull out your mobile phone and look at it?

Do you long to be in heaven? Let God stoke up the holy longing to be with him and to know him better. It will only be fully satisfied when you die or Jesus returns, but its purpose is to propel you onwards and upwards in your Ascent, to encourage you to persevere though the hard times in the certain hope of the glory that is to come. One day you will see him face to face and have your own special room in heaven.

SOME BIBLE VERSES TO MEDITATE ON

This is eternal life: that they may know you, the only true God, and Jesus Christ, whom you have sent.

John 17:3

Father, I want those you have given me to be with me where I am and to see my glory.

John 17:24

I desire to depart and be with Christ, which is better by far.

Philippians 1:23

My Father's house has many rooms; if that were not so, would I have told you that I am going there to prepare a place for you?

John 14:2

"Yes, I am coming soon." Amen. Come, Lord Jesus.

Revelation 22:20

12

Together in battle

Some of the deepest relationships are made in battle. I have never lived through a war, but I can see that there is a special bond between those who have fought together. They have seen friends wounded and killed, shared the anxiety of waiting and endured together the intensity of conflict.

The battle as a Christian takes many forms. I have identified four:

- we battle for holiness and against sin in our lives;
- we strive for love and unity in the church;
- we endure suffering and persecution; and
- we labour to take the good news about Jesus to the ends of the earth, often at great cost, through our words and our deeds of love in Jesus' name.

Jesus knew what it was to be alone in his most intense conflict. He promises that he will never leave us in the way that his disciples left him. More than that, he intends that we should have brothers and sisters to stand alongside us so that we battle together. We will emerge with our relationships deepened, both with others and with God himself.

Application

Jesus warns you of the tough times that lie ahead and equips you with his Holy Spirit to be able to overcome. He does not send you out alone, but to work with others, relying on their friendship, support and partnership. Reflect on the state of the battles in your life, against sin, within the church, enduring suffering and sharing the good news about Jesus. Thank God for the support you have in each of your battles.

Jesus stands shoulder to shoulder with you in each of these conflicts. Rely on his promises. Pray that God will equip you. Pray daily for the filling of his Holy Spirit, for purity and power, for compassion and for courage. Know that he is with you whatever happens and that he will never leave you nor forsake you.

As you complete the Ascent, remember that God loves you and that you will be with him forever. Use this book as a journey in your imagination that allows you to draw closer to God as you travel through your life with him. Keep trusting, serving and obeying him, looking forward to that day when he says to you, "Well done, good and faithful servant."[14]

SOME BIBLE VERSES TO MEDITATE ON

The Lord is with you, mighty warrior ... Go in the strength you have ... Am I not sending you? ... I will be with you.

Judges 6:12-16

Be strong in the Lord and in his mighty power. Put on the full armour of God so that you can take your stand against the devil's schemes.

Ephesians 6:10-11

In this world you will have trouble. But take heart! I have overcome the world.

John 16:33

In all these things we are more than conquerors through him who loved us.

Romans 8:37

Never will I leave you; never will I forsake you.

Hebrews 13:5

---

[14] Matthew 25:21

Author's Note

If this book has encouraged you to want to know Jesus for the first time, you can join an Alpha Course[15] or go to:

www.allaboutgod.com/how-to-become-a-christian.htm

If you want to contact me and discuss anything in the book, then write to:

theascentpg@gmail.com

---

[15] You can find details of an Alpha Course in your area at *http://alpha.org*

Similar Books from the Publisher

Feasting on the Father
William L. Smith
ISBN 978-1-907509-34-6

The Bible is essentially a love story – a book that reveals the heart of a Father towards his children. God does not keep his distance from us, nor is it his desire to punish us. On the contrary, his love compelled him to send his only son into an imbalanced world – to suffer in our place, and to bring us back to the Father as royal sons. Now, we are welcome to the table of the King of Kings... The truths explained in this book have the power to change your life. Once you have feasted on the Father, you will not want to look back...

The Undivided Heart
Florence J. Joseph
ISBN 978-1-910197-30-1

Interspersed with humour, anecdotes, poems and stories, this book describes the journey, from its origins in God, through the broken and damaged places of our hearts, into the love of the Father and our place in His heart. It is an invitation to engage deeply with our own heart issues, and so be better able to communicate with Him and with others from a place of understanding, depth and generosity. Reading and applying this book is like taking a tonic that will leave you feeling refreshed and restored.

Books available from all good bookshops and from the publisher:
www.onwardsandupwards.org